WORLD HISTORY   500 B.C. – A.D. 500

Ancient
ROME

TOPS K-8

PICTURE CREDITS
Cover Paul Almasy/Corbis; pages 1, 3 bottom, 4–5, 25, 43 bottom, 45 left, 56 Erich Lessing/Art Resource, NY; pages 3 top, 6, 50 left, 55 Araldo de Luca/Corbis; pages 3 middle bottom, 28 Lloyd Kenneth Townsend Jr./National Geographic Image Collection; pages 3 middle top, 36–37 Image Bank/Getty Images; pages 8, 9 middle, 24, 44 Scala/Art Resource, NY; page 9 top Jonathan S. Blair/National Geographic Image Collection; page 9 bottom Vanni/Art Resource, NY; pages 10–11, 13 Painting by Peter V. Bianchi/National Geographic Image Collection; page 14 Charles and Josette Lenars/Corbis; pages 16–17 Peter Essick/National Geographic Image Collection; pages 18, 57 bottom Leslie Garland Picture Library/Alamy Images; page 19 left The Art Archive/Dagli Orti; page 19 right Jonathan Blair/Corbis; page 19 bottom Chase Swift/Corbis; page 20 top Christopher A. Klein/National Geographic Image Collection; pages 20 bottom, 50 middle right, 57 top O. Louis Mazzatenta/National Geographic Image Collection; pages 22–23 Robert Harding Picture Library/Alamy Images; pages 26–27 The Art Archive/Galleria Borghese Rome/Dagli Orti; pages 27, 50 top left The Art Archive/Archaeological Museum Naples/Dagli Orti; page 29 Dreamworks/Universal/The Kobal Collection/Buitendijk, Jaap; pages 30–31, 38, 47, 50 top right James A. Stanfield/National Geographic Image Collection; pages 32–33 The Art Archive/San Gennaro Catacombs Naples Italy/Dagli Orti; pages 34, 58, 63 Giraudon/Art Resource, NY; page 35 Louvre, Paris, France/Peter Willi/Bridgeman Art Library; page 36 The Art Archive/National Museum Bucharest/Dagli Orti; page 39 Patrick Ward/Corbis; pages 40–41 Ross Ressmeyer/Corbis; page 42 left Werner Forman/Art Resource, NY; page 42 right Borromeo/Art Resource, NY; page 43 left Alinari/Art Resource, NY; page 45 right Mimmo Jodice/Corbis; page 48 top Don Maitz/National Geographic Image Collection; page 49 Philip Gould/Corbis; page 50 middle right Richard T. Nowitz/Corbis; page 50 bottom left, 57 right The Granger Collection; page 50 bottom right Museo Archaeologico Nazionale, Naples, Italy/Alinari/Bridgeman Art Library; page 51 Dennis Degnan/Corbis; page 52 Craig Aurness/Corbis; pages 53, 62 Bettmann/Corbis; page 59 Walters Art Museum, Baltimore, USA/Bridgeman Art Library; page 60 Gilles Mermet / Art Resource, NY; page 61 top The Art Archive/Basilica Aquileia Italy/Dagli Orti; page 61 bottom Private Collection/Bridgeman Art Library.

Produced through the worldwide resources of the National Geographic Society, John M. Fahey, Jr., President and Chief Executive Officer; Gilbert M. Grosvenor, Chairman of the Board; Nina D. Hoffman, Executive Vice President and President, Books and Education Publishing Group.

PREPARED BY NATIONAL GEOGRAPHIC SCHOOL PUBLISHING
Ericka Markman, Senior Vice President and President Children's Books and Education Publishing Group; Steve Mico, Senior Vice President, Editorial Director; Marianne Hiland, Executive Editor; Richard Easby, Editorial Manager; Anita Schwartz, Project Editor; Jim Hiscott, Design Manager; Kristin Hanneman, Illustrations Manager; Matt Wascavage, Manager of Publishing Services; Sean Philpotts, Production Manager; Jane Ponton, Production Artist.

MANUFACTURING AND QUALITY CONTROL
Christopher A. Liedel, Chief Financial Officer; Phillip L. Schlosser, Director; Clifton M. Brown III, Manager.

ART DIRECTION Dan Banks, Project Design Company

CONSULTANT/REVIEWER
Dr. Andrew M. Riggsby, Associate Professor of Classics, University of Texas at Austin

BOOK DEVELOPMENT Nieman Inc.

BOOK DESIGN Three Communication Design, LLC

PICTURE EDITING Paula McLeod, Worth a Thousand Words, Inc.

MAP DEVELOPMENT AND PRODUCTION Mapping Specialists, Ltd.

Published by the National Geographic Society
1145 17th Street, N.W.
Washington, D.C. 20036-4688

ISBN-13: 978-0-7922-4943-6
ISBN-10: 0-7922-4943-7

Third Printing June, 2012
Printed in Canada

cover: Roman theater in Spain **page 1:** Bronze Roman helmet **page 3** (top): Statue of the emperor Augustus **page 3** (center right): Modern painting of lions at the Colosseum **page 3** (center left): Hadrian's Wall in Britain **page 3** (bottom): Roman panel showing chariot race

4 INTRODUCTION

26

36

56 OVERVIEW

Ancient
ROME

From a tiny city-state in central Italy, Rome grew into one of the largest and most enduring empires in history. The legacy of this ancient empire lives on in our language, laws, roads, and buildings.

This ruins of the Forum survive in Rome. The Forum was the main marketplace in ancient Rome, where the Romans conducted business, listened to political speeches, and met their friends.

ACCORDING TO ROMAN LEGEND, Rome was founded in 753 B.C. The ancient Romans built their city on seven hills near Italy's Tiber River. Rome's location helped it survive and grow. Built on hills, the city was easy to defend. Italy had a good climate and enough fertile land to feed a large population. The Tiber gave the city a link to the sea for both trade and conquest.

The early history of Rome was a long struggle against neighboring peoples, such as the Etruscans, who lived north of Rome. In 509 B.C., the Romans overthrew the king who ruled them and set up a **republic,** a form of government in which citizens elect their leaders. By about 272 B.C., Rome controlled most of Italy.

Augustus Caesar, Rome's first emperor

Length of Recorded History

3000 B.C. Writing invented

509 B.C.
Founding of the Roman Republic

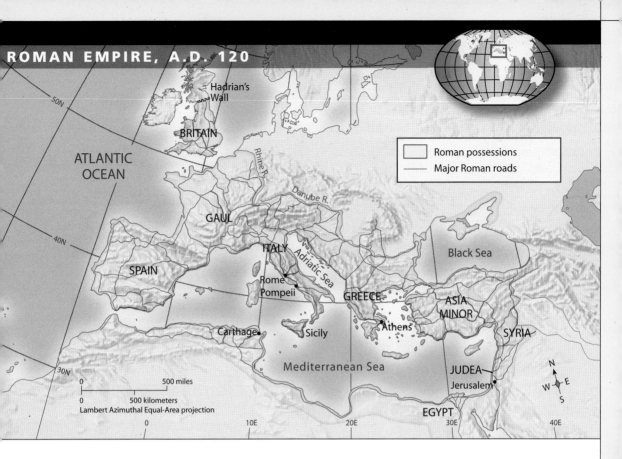

Roman possessions

Major Roman roads

50N

Hadrian's Wall

BRITAIN

ATLANTIC OCEAN

Rhine R.

Danube R.

GAUL

40N

ITALY

Adriatic Sea

Black Sea

SPAIN

Rome

Pompeii

GREECE

ASIA MINOR

Carthage

Sicily

Athens

SYRIA

30N

Mediterranean Sea

JUDEA

Jerusalem

EGYPT

0   500 miles

0   500 kilometers

Lambert Azimuthal Equal-Area projection

10E   20E   30E   40E

N W E S

During the next 400 years, the Romans conquered an area about the size of the present-day United States. At its height about A.D. 120, the Roman Empire included most of Europe, the coast of North Africa, and a large part of the Middle East. The entire coastline of the Mediterranean Sea was Roman. The Romans called the Mediterranean *mare nostrum,* "our sea."

One major factor in Rome's success was the skill and organization of the Roman army. Another was the vast network of paved roads that tied Rome's huge empire together.

A.D. 1   A.D. 2000

A.D. 476
Fall of the Roman Empire

Ancient Rome   7

As the Roman Empire grew, new power and wealth brought Rome new problems. Large numbers of landless farmers and other poor people swelled the city's population. To control public unrest, Roman rulers provided them with free food and brutal spectacles, such as chariot races and combats between professional fighters known as gladiators.

Another challenge to Rome was the arrival of a new religion. Between about A.D. 40 and 100, Christianity spread throughout the Roman Empire. At times, Roman officials tried to stop the new faith's spread by mistreating or killing Christians. This ended in A.D. 313, when the Roman ruler Constantine granted all people in the empire freedom of worship.

As the empire expanded, the Romans struggled to defend their borders. In some places, border walls were built to keep out "barbarian" peoples from beyond the empire. In A.D. 285, the Roman ruler split the empire into eastern and western parts to make governing it more manageable.

By the late 300s, the Western Roman Empire was beginning to collapse under a series of barbarian invasions. One group of invaders seized power in A.D. 476, a date usually seen as the fall of the Western Roman Empire.

The articles in this book describe how the city of Rome grew to be a great empire and created a civilization that has had an enduring influence. To help guide your reading, they have been organized around the following three **BIG IDEAS:**

1 Military power helped Rome grow from a small city-state to a great empire.

2 Rome faced challenges from both inside and outside the empire.

3 Rome created a powerful, enduring civilization that continues to influence and fascinate people today.

As you read, keep these ideas in mind. They will help you understand the most important characteristics and achievements of ancient Rome.

BIG IDEA: THE RISE OF ROME

The courage and discipline of Roman soldiers made them a powerful fighting force.

BIG IDEA: CHALLENGES TO THE EMPIRE

The peace and order of the Roman world made it possible for Christianity to spread rapidly.

BIG IDEA: THE LEGACY OF ROME

The grandeur of Roman buildings served as a model for later Western architecture.

The army of the
Carthaginian general
Hannibal crossed the
Alps to attack Rome's
homeland of Italy.

CARTHA
MUST BE
DESI

A restless drive to power spurred Rome's growth. As soon as all of Italy was theirs, the Romans looked for new conquests. Standing in their way was another expanding empire, Carthage.

GE

ROYED!

Geography was at the root of the conflict between Rome and Carthage. These two powerful, ambitious groups faced each other across the Mediterranean Sea. Between 264 and 146 B.C., they fought three wars, called the Punic Wars, for control of Mediterranean territories. Each growing empire wished to control the valuable trade and resources of the region. Rome and Carthage fought the First Punic War for control of the rich island of Sicily, which lay between them. Rome won, and Sicily became the first Roman **province**, or division of the Roman Empire.

The Carthaginians wanted to avenge this defeat. Their greatest general, Hamilcar Barca, had his three sons swear an oath that they would never give up the struggle with Rome. Hamilcar's eldest son, Hannibal, took his father's words to heart.

Carthage ruled an area that included southern Spain. From there, Hannibal launched the Second Punic War against Rome in 218 B.C. Gathering an army of foot soldiers, horsemen, and 60 war elephants, he marched north and east into France. His forces crossed the Rhône River on rafts. They struggled through the Alps, fighting cold, landslides, and attacks by mountain peoples. By the time they reached northern Italy, only one elephant was left.

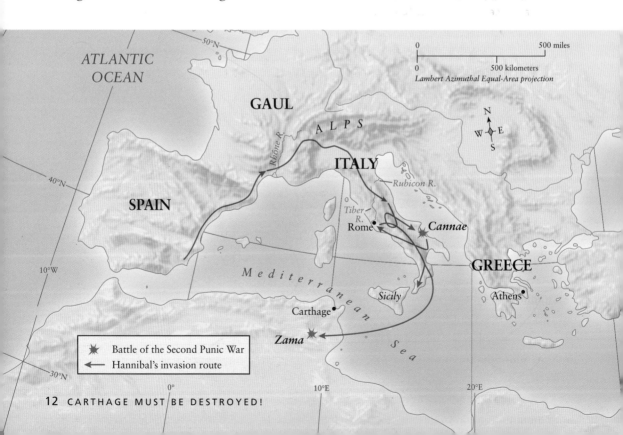

★ Battle of the Second Punic War
← Hannibal's invasion route

Hannibal's Victory at Cannae

Hannibal crushed the Roman armies sent against him. After resting his troops, he marched toward Rome. Determined to stop Hannibal, the Romans sent out an army of 86,000 men, the largest force they had ever assembled. The two armies met in early August, 216 B.C., at the town of Cannae (KAN–ee) in southeastern Italy.

Knowing that Roman forces usually attacked the center of the enemy's line, Hannibal set a trap. Forming his troops into an arc, he allowed the central portion of his men to retreat ahead of the Romans. The two sides of the arc swung around them. Surrounded and packed together so tightly they could barely swing their swords, the Romans fought and died, row by row.

Cannae was the worst defeat Rome ever suffered. How bad was it? Only high-ranking Romans wore gold signet rings. After the battle, Hannibal's men filled three large baskets with gold rings taken from dead Romans.

Hannibal hoped his victories would make Rome's allies join his side, but few did. As a result, he did not have sufficient forces to capture the city of Rome itself.

At Cannae, Hannibal destroyed most of the huge Roman army sent against his forces.

Rome's Revenge at Zama

The Romans decided to take the war to the Carthaginians. First, they spent ten years conquering Spain. Next, they invaded North Africa. This strategy forced Hannibal and his army to leave Italy and return to defend their home. In 202 B.C., the Roman general Scipio (SIP–ee–oh) fought Hannibal on the plains of Zama southwest of Carthage.

Both armies had between 35,000 and 40,000 men. Hannibal had war elephants, but Scipio had better foot soldiers and horsemen. The elephants charged into the Romans. But the soldiers shouted and made enough noise to scare the beasts, causing them to run off in all directions. Some even ran back into the Carthaginian army.

The End of Carthage

With this defeat, Carthage was forced to give up territory in Spain and Africa and make huge payments to Rome for 50 years. But some Roman leaders feared that Carthage might again threaten Rome. In the **Senate,** the supreme council of state in the Roman Republic, Senator Cato finished every speech by shouting "Carthage must be destroyed!" He finally goaded Rome into a third war with Carthage in 149 B.C. Carthage resisted a Roman attack—led by Scipio's grandson—for three years. Finally, the Romans succeeded in capturing Carthage and burning the city. Carthage was destroyed.

Roman soldiers charge in formation at a historical re-enactment.

The Roman Army

The Romans could never have succeeded without the Roman army, one of the most effective military forces in history. In the early days of the Republic, only landowning citizens of Rome were soldiers. But as their empire expanded, the Romans started using recruits from conquered provinces. After 20 years of service, these recruits could become citizens of Rome. By the first century A.D., Rome had about 300,000 troops, most of them from the provinces outside Rome.

The Roman army was organized into groups called **legions**. Each legion was commanded by a general and six officers known as tribunes.

At full strength, each legion consisted of 10 **cohorts** of about 480 men each. A cohort was formed of six **centuries** of 80 to 100 men each, commanded by a centurion.

Roman soldiers—called legionaries—were professionals who made soldiering their careers. They served between 16 and 26 years depending on rank. Legionaries used javelins and swords in battle. They protected themselves with wooden shields rimmed with iron.

When not actively at war, Roman soldiers built roads, bridges, **aqueducts** (channels used to carry water), walls, and forts. Living most of their lives in the provinces, legionaries often married local women and settled down. They spread Roman culture throughout Europe, North Africa, and the Middle East.

▶ *For more information about the Roman army and the Punic Wars, see page 58.*

▶ *see page 58.*

STRUCTURE OF THE ROMAN ARMY

1 LEGION

10 COHORTS
480 MEN IN EACH

6 CENTURIES
80–100 MEN IN EACH

WHY IT MATTERS TODAY

Geography influences history. The growth of their empires caused Rome and Carthage to go to war for control of the Mediterranean. Today, conflicts continue to arise as nations, tribes, and other groups struggle over territory.

An important factor in the Romans' success as empire builders was their success as roadbuilders. Over a vast network of roads, Roman armies marched to battle and goods reached markets.

ALL ROADS LEAD TO ROM

Surfaced with carefully fitted stone blocks, many Roman roads have lasted more than 2,000 years.

E

According to a famous saying, "All roads lead to Rome." In the time of the ancient Romans, this just stated a fact. The Romans built roads linking the most distant parts of the lands they ruled. They built their roads to last. If you visit parts of Europe and the Middle East today, you can still see Roman roads that are nearly 2,000 years old.

The Romans constructed more than 370 main roads covering over 50,000 miles (80,000 kilometers). Originally, the Romans built the roads so that their armies could move quickly. However, the Roman road system soon became a critical part of a network of trade routes. Across land and sea, the wealth of places near and far reached Rome.

The economy of the ancient Romans could not have functioned without their system of roads.

Built to Last

Since roads were so important to Rome's defense and prosperity, the Romans built them very carefully. This was especially true when they constructed one of the *viae publicae* ("public ways"), the first-class highways maintained by the Roman state. To construct a main road, workers first dug a trench. They packed down the soil and covered it with crushed stones to help water drain. Over this, they put a layer of sand, or gravel and sand, to strengthen the road. The top layer was the road surface itself, made of carefully fitted stone blocks.

A Roman bridge still used in Switzerland

TWO HIGHWAY SYSTEMS

FEATURE	ROMAN ROADS	U.S. INTERSTATES
Total mileage of system	More than 50,000 miles (80,000 kilometers)	About 43,000 miles (69,000 kilometers)
First major highway	Via Appia between Rome and the Italian port of Brindisi, begun in 312 B.C.	Lincoln Highway between New York City and San Francisco, begun in 1913
Road width	Varied greatly from main roads to local roads	Minimum of two lanes in each direction
Construction materials	Broken stones, sand, gravel, stone blocks	Concrete, asphalt, gravel
Travel restrictions	In the city of Rome, hours of use and cargo weight for carts	Speed limits and cargo weight for trucks
Special structures	Stone bridges with pillars and arches, tunnels, causeways (elevated roads over water or wet ground)	Steel and concrete bridges with pillars or suspension cables, tunnels, causeways
Aids for travelers	Milestones, inns	Mileage signs, rest areas

SPEED LIMIT 55

THE GOLDEN
MILESTONE

In 20 B.C., Augustus, the first Roman emperor, erected the *Milliarium Aureum*, or "Golden Milestone," in the center of Rome. This bronze column listed the mileage between Rome and the principal cities of the Roman Empire.

A Roman road was built in several layers (top).

Only the base of the Milliarium Aureum survives (bottom).

Roads were built higher in the middle and lower on the sides to help water run off. Gutters, curbs, and footpaths lined the roadsides. Whenever possible, the Romans built their roads in straight lines. They constructed tunnels and bridges so the roads could follow the most direct routes between places.

The Queen of Roads

The Via Appia, or Appian Way, was the first and most famous of Rome's long-distance military-commercial highways. A Roman poet called it "the Queen of Roads." The Appian Way was begun in 312 B.C., and named for Appius Claudius, the Roman official who started it. It originally was a military road that ran 132 miles (212 kilometers) south from Rome to the town of Capua. Later, it was extended another 230 miles (370 kilometers) further south and then east to the city of Brundisium on the Adriatic Sea. Being linked to Rome by the Appian Way transformed Brundisium (present-day Brindisi) into one of the most important seaports in the Roman Empire.

At one spot, the Appian Way had to cross a wide stretch of marshland. First, the Roman road builders drained part of the marshes. Then they hammered heavy timbers into the ground and filled in around them with stone rubble.

On top of this, they put the layered bed of the Appian Way—a tremendous engineering feat. Few other ancient peoples knew how to make roadbeds at all, let alone across swamps.

On the Road

Most of those who traveled the Roman roads went on foot. Richer people used carriages or wagons pulled by horses or mules. Inns along the way offered beds and food for travelers and stables for their animals. Other travelers rented a room in a private home.

Long journeys over Roman roads were not easy. One traveler on the Appian Way complained of greedy innkeepers, bad drinking water, and mosquitoes that kept him awake at night. Despite the difficulties, Roman roads helped hold the empire together.

▶ *For more information about how Rome kept its empire unified, see pages 60–61.*

WHY IT MATTERS TODAY

Highway systems today play an essential part in the military planning and economic life of modern nations. They are part of the infrastructure, the basic facilities that enable communities to function. These include systems that provide water, power, transportation, communication, and sanitation.

Julius Caesar

The skill and ambition of Rome's military leaders was both a blessing and a curse. Their victories brought new wealth and power to Rome, but their violent rivalries destroyed the Roman Republic.

HAIL, CAESAR!

On January 10, 49 B.C., a Roman general named Julius Caesar stood in front of 5,000 Roman soldiers. They were near the Rubicon, a small river marking the boundary of the Roman province that Caesar governed. He wanted to return to Rome to run for office. He had plans for reform that he intended to put into action.

In the last years of the republic, the Roman Senate faced many attempts to seize power. Here, the Roman leader Cicero (standing left) delivers a famous speech denouncing the conspiracy of the Roman politician Catiline (alone at the right) to overthrow the government.

The Roman Senate had ordered Caesar not to bring his army back to Rome. Some of them feared he would use his army to take over the government. But with enemies waiting for him in Rome, Caesar knew he needed his troops. On the banks of the Rubicon, Caesar's army waited for his signal. Galloping over the bridge, he shouted, "The die is cast!" He meant that he was ready to risk everything, as on a roll of the dice. Caesar's troops followed him across the river. There was no going back now, for Caesar or for Rome.

The End of the Republic

Caesar's chief rival for power in Rome was a general named Pompey. Pompey and Caesar had once been political partners, but now they were enemies. When Caesar marched on Rome, he defeated Pompey's armies and others that rose against him. The Roman Senate made him **dictator,** or absolute ruler. In the past, Roman dictators had ruled for six months, in times of emergency. But in 45 B.C., Caesar was named dictator-for-life.

CAESAR BY ANOTHER NAME

Although only the first few Roman emperors were actually related to Julius Caesar, all of them used his family name as a title. From then on, the name *Caesar* referred to a supreme ruler. The titles *kaiser* (for the ruler of the German Empire) and *czar* (for the ruler of the Russian Empire) both came from *Caesar.*

Coronation of Czar Nicholas II and Empress Alexandra of Russia

Caesar quickly put his reform plans into action. He expanded the Senate from 300 to 900 members. He granted citizenship to some foreigners living in Rome. He created jobs for the poor, especially in the construction of new public buildings. He increased pay for soldiers and established areas where the landless poor could have farms. He even changed the calendar, creating the one on which our current calendar is based. He did not have time to do much more. On March 15, 44 B.C., a small group of senators, hating his complete control of power, stabbed him to death.

Those who murdered Caesar hoped to bring back the republic, but it was not to be. A new struggle for power ended when Caesar's nephew and adopted son Octavian became Rome's supreme ruler. In 27 B.C., the Senate gave him the title of *Augustus,* the "revered one." Later, he received the title *imperator,* or emperor. Although Augustus gave some power to the Senate, it was largely for show. In reality, the Roman Republic had ended, and the empire, governed by individual rulers, had begun.

▶ *For more information about Rome's civil war and Julius Caesar, see page 59.*

WHY IT MATTERS TODAY

Brutal struggles for power between rival military leaders have shaped the history of many parts of the world in modern times. As in ancient Rome, these conflicts often destroy representative government in the process.

MELITIO

A gladiator fights a wild
beast in the arena.

BREAD &

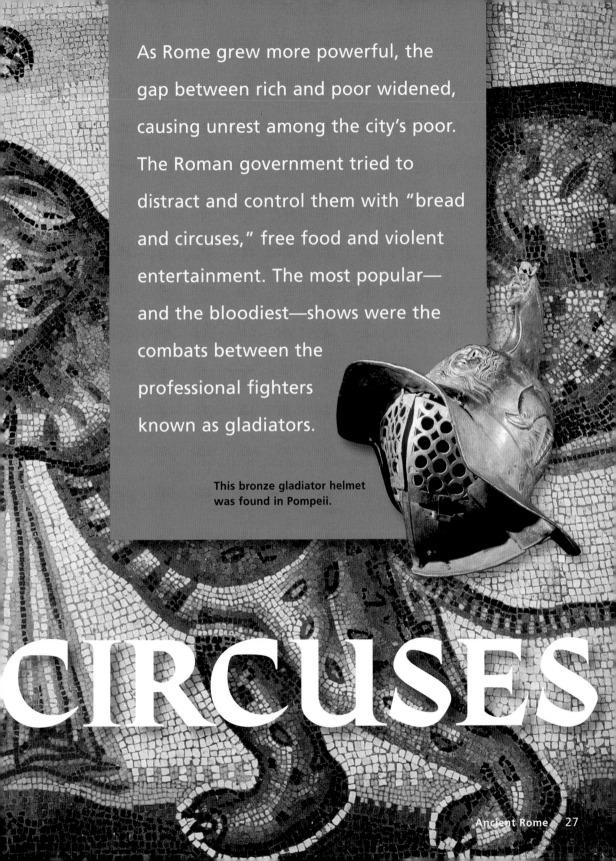

As Rome grew more powerful, the gap between rich and poor widened, causing unrest among the city's poor. The Roman government tried to distract and control them with "bread and circuses," free food and violent entertainment. The most popular— and the bloodiest—shows were the combats between the professional fighters known as gladiators.

This bronze gladiator helmet was found in Pompeii.

CIRCUSES

Lions pace as gladiators await them in the arena.

We have all seen them at the movies. They stride out into the glare of the arena grasping their swords and spears. Screaming for blood, nearly 50,000 Romans rise from their seats. The fighters stand beneath the emperor's box. Lifting their weapons, they shout, "Hail, Caesar! We who are about to die, salute you!" They are gladiators.

The Latin word *gladiator* comes from *gladius*, which means "sword." Many gladiators did fight using a short sword. Others were armed with curved swords or long spears. Some carried a three-pointed spear (called a trident) and a net. Others fought riding horses or chariots. Many of the different types of weapons, armor, and fighting styles were those of enemies the Romans had met in battle.

Most gladiators were criminals, slaves, or captured prisoners from all over the Roman Empire. These men had no choice but to fight. Some free men who were down on their luck actually volunteered to be gladiators and face probable death.

According to legend, if a wounded gladiator was still alive at the end of a match, the emperor decided his fate based on the wishes of the crowd. The thumbs up sign meant that the wounded man might live to fight another day. Thumbs down condemned him to death. If he had shown courage during the fight, the gladiator would probably live.

The World's Bloodiest Sport

The citizens of ancient Rome were serious about having fun. They lived for good food and parties. They loved hearing musicians play. But watching deadly combats in the Colosseum was also a very popular pastime. This amphitheater was built especially for huge gladiator spectacles. The arena's wooden floor was covered with sand to soak up the blood spilled in the fights. On the Colosseum's opening day in A.D. 80, bloodthirsty crowds watched more than 5,000 animals killed. Roman emperors presented these shows to keep people happy.

Some emperors were such fans of the gladiator combats that they entered the arena themselves. The emperor Commodus fought more than 1,000 men and never lost a match. Did he succeed because of his skill or the fact that his opponents were afraid to defeat the emperor?

Commodus also liked to participate in the brutal animal shows. A typical day at the Colosseum would begin with a massive roundup of caged wild animals. Lions, leopards, bears, elephants, and other animals were let loose to kill each other or be killed by men who were forced into the arena with them.

PAST TO PRESENT

LIGHTS! CAMERA! BLOOD!

From the earliest days of silent movies, Hollywood filmmakers have enjoyed creating epic stories of ancient Rome. Spectacular gladiator combats and chariot races are among the most memorable moments in these films. Here actor Russell Crowe (right) plays a gladiator in the 2000 film *Gladiator.*

These gladiators carry different weapons, but each wears an armored sleeve, or *manica*.

In order to supply the animals needed for these shows, the Romans developed a trade in wild beasts. As a result, some types of animals—such as elephants, hippos, and lions—almost disappeared from parts of the empire where they had been common.

The decline of the Roman Empire eventually led to the end of the gladiator combats. The money and resources needed to stage the spectacles were no longer available. The new Christian religion was becoming more popular among the Roman people. The Christian teachings of peace and love seemed to conflict with the terrifying displays in the Colosseum.

In A.D. 312, the emperor Constantine passed laws against the gladiator contests. But it took 80 more years to stop the games completely. In A.D. 404, a Christian monk jumped into an arena

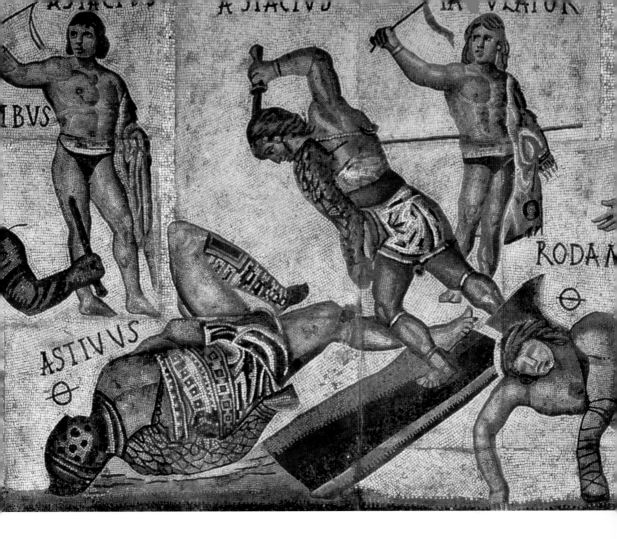

in Rome and tried to stop two gladiators from killing each other. The angry crowd climbed over the barricades and brutally killed the monk. In response, the emperor Honorius banned all gladiator fights. The world's bloodiest sport had finally come to an end.

▶ *For more information about Christianity and the decline of the empire, see pages 58–59.*

For more information about Christianity and the decline of the empire, see pages 58–59.

WHY IT MATTERS TODAY

The ancient Romans valued the qualities of warriors, such as strength and courage. This led both to the greatness of the Roman army and to the brutality of the gladiator combats. The gladiators of ancient Rome remain one of the most grimly fascinating parts of Roman culture for people today.

In an ancient tomb painting, an early Christian raises her hands in prayer.

A New Faith

The Romans were generally tolerant of all the religions in their empire. But because the early Christians refused to participate in the official worship of the Roman gods, Roman rulers sometimes treated them cruelly.

Tacitus, a famous Roman historian, called Christianity a "deadly superstition." The new religion had originally appeared in the Roman province of Judea. Soon, Christianity had spread to the city of Rome. In Rome, Tacitus complained, "all things horrible and shameful in the world collect and become popular."

The Roman Empire was enormous, containing millions of people from vastly different cultures. In order to unify this empire, the Romans encouraged the people they had conquered to worship the Roman gods. For cultures that already worshiped many gods, adding the Roman ones was not a problem.

The Romans themselves adopted gods from other cultures, particularly the Greek gods. As long as people respected the Roman gods and honored the emperor as Rome's chief priest, they could follow their own religion.

The Christians, however, refused to honor Roman gods. Even more insulting to the Romans, they were outspoken about it. They said that their god was the only real one. As a result, the Romans mistrusted the Christian religion. They often accused Christians of crimes and of practicing black magic.

Suspicion soon erupted into violence in A.D. 64. A disastrous fire destroyed a great part of Rome. Although some Romans believed that the emperor Nero himself had started the fire, he blamed the fire on the Christians. He rounded up hundreds of Christians and sent them to the public arena. There, according to a Roman historian, "mockery of every sort was added to their death. Covered with the skins of beasts, they were torn by dogs and perished, or were nailed to crosses, or were doomed to the flames."

A disastrous fire destroyed a great part of Rome.

On the night of July 19, A.D. 64, a fire broke out in Rome. Nine days later, two-thirds of the city was a smoking ruin.

Christianity Spreads

Despite these horrors, Christianity continued to spread. In A.D. 95, the Roman emperor responded by making the "false religion" illegal. Over the next 150 years, Christians suffered outbreaks of mob violence against them. Yet the religion continued to grow, in part because of the work of **missionaries**, people who work to spread word of a faith.

Constantine

In A.D. 250, the Roman emperor launched a campaign to ensure that all Roman subjects made sacrifices to the Roman gods. Since the Christians refused to obey, the result was **persecution** of Christians throughout the empire. Over the next few years, many Christian leaders were arrested and executed. Christian Roman citizens were stripped of their status, or social position, and property. Others were enslaved.

Another round of persecutions began in A.D. 303. The emperor Diocletian (di–uh–KLEE–shuhn) ordered all Christian scriptures, or writings, to be burned, and all Christian churches destroyed. Meetings for Christian worship were forbidden. Christian priests were deported or killed.

Despite all these measures, Christianity continued to survive and attract converts. The religion appealed to all kinds of people because of its messages of equality and compassion. In the end, the policy of the Roman government toward Christianity changed. In A.D. 313, the emperor Constantine issued an order granting "both to the Christians and to all men freedom to follow the religion they choose." Toleration soon became support. About A.D. 392, the emperor Theodosius (thee–uh–DOH–shuhs) made Christianity the official religion of the Roman Empire.

▶ *For more information about the spread of Christianity, see page 61.*

WHY IT MATTERS TODAY

As the state religion of the Roman Empire, Christianity vastly expanded its base of followers. It became the dominant religion of Europe, and later of the parts of the world settled by Europeans, such as North and South America. About two billion people around the world practice Christianity today.

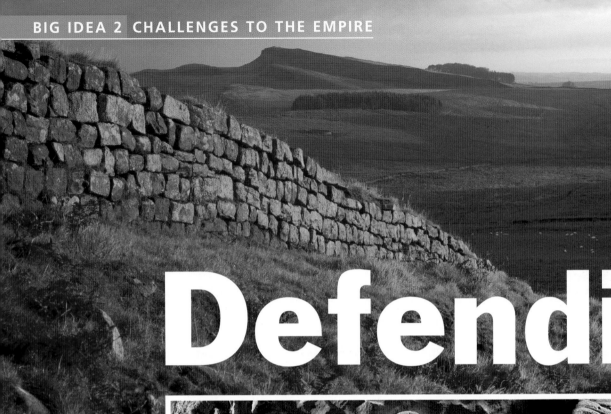

Defendi

Hadrian's Wall snaking across the countryside of northern England (top)

Roman troops building a wall (bottom)

ng the WALL

As the boundaries of the empire expanded, Roman soldiers found themselves stationed at distant, uncomfortable, lonely, often dangerous outposts. Some of these were forts along Hadrian's Wall, the northern boundary of the Roman province of Britain.

A soldier, shivering in a gray, cold wind, stands guard over a wall in Britain, the northern boundary of the Roman Empire. He pulls his cloak tightly about him and dreams of home. The soldier is helping to protect the Roman army's greatest achievement—Hadrian's Wall.

The expansion of the Roman Empire created problems. The more distant the empire's borders grew, the harder it was to protect them. Sending additional troops from Rome to distant provinces was rarely worth the trouble. This was especially true in areas with small populations, such as northern Britain. The money spent defending the local people there was greater than the small amount of taxes collected from them.

One way to cut costs was to use **auxiliaries** (awg–ZIL–yuh–rees), soldiers recruited from the lands the Romans had conquered. Though paid less than the legionaries, Rome's regular soldiers, auxiliaries worked for a more important reward. After 20 years, they became citizens of the empire, a rank their families could enjoy in the future.

Another way to cut expenses was to avoid conflict in the first place. This was part of the reason for building Hadrian's Wall. The wall extends 73 miles (117 kilometers), from coast to coast, across the narrow neck of northern Britain. Its purpose was to keep people farther north from making raids into Roman territory. Earlier emperors had unsuccessfully tried to conquer these tribes.

Roman  Citizens

In most of the ancient world you inherited citizenship—just like a family name. The Romans generally followed this rule, but created some exceptions so that non-Romans could get Roman citizenship. For example, slaves freed by Roman owners became Romans themselves. Citizenship could also be given to reward foreigners who helped Rome in some way. This was automatic for auxiliaries under the Empire.

In A.D. 212, all free inhabitants of the empire were made citizens.

Under the Republic, only male citizens could vote and hold office. Citizens were free from arbitrary punishment by government officials. Roman law only recognized wills in which citizens left their property to other citizens. It did not recognize marriage between a citizen and a non-citizen.

Milecastle along Hadrian's Wall

At a few key points along the wall, major forts housed several hundred legionaries. Every mile, however, there were much smaller outposts called "milecastles." Between these were watchtowers from which auxiliaries could search the landscape for trouble. The distance between these watchtowers could be reached by foot in less than three minutes. By using a kind of relay race, auxiliaries kept news traveling quickly along the wall. They also did whatever was necessary to maintain the wall and the forces defending it. This could mean anything from digging a ditch to building a small hospital.

The wall was in use until the late 400s, when the Romans left Britain. Much of it was then destroyed by invading tribes who used the stone as foundations for their homes. However, its ruins still snake across northern Britain, as proof of its builders' exceptional abilities.

When Hadrian became emperor in A.D. 117, he realized that a strong defense was more sensible. The building of the wall in A.D. 122 helped defend the empire's northern border.

▶ *For more information about the division and decline of the Roman Empire, see pages 61–62.*

Building the Wall

Starting on the east coast and working westward, Roman soldiers built closely parallel rows of stone walls. Then they filled in the gaps with cheaper materials such as sand and clay. For most of its length, Hadrian's Wall was 12 feet (3.7 meters) high and 8 feet (2.4 meters) wide. Auxiliaries transported most of the several million tons of stone used.

WHY IT MATTERS TODAY

The ruins of Hadrian's Wall show that the Romans set limits to the growth of their empire. Today, countries establish borders to maintain security, control immigration, and regulate trade.

TIME
CAPSULE

A.D. 79

The eruption of Mount Vesuvius in A.D. 79 buried the small Roman city of Pompeii. Forgotten for many centuries and rediscovered by chance, Pompeii has provided a glimpse into the lost world of ancient Rome.

The last moments of a resident of Pompeii were preserved by the volcanic ash that killed him.

The people of Pompeii enjoyed bright colors, from the painted walls of their houses (left) to everyday objects such as this glass pitcher and bowl (below).

Pompeii (pom–PAY) was a pleasant Roman town near the Bay of Naples. To the people of Pompeii, their neighbor Mount Vesuvius had always been just pretty scenery. Then, on August 24, A.D. 79, a roar shattered the quiet, the earth shook, and Vesuvius exploded. Buried under a thick layer of volcanic ash, Pompeii became a lost city.

We know the moment when Mount Vesuvius erupted because of two letters that give an eyewitness account of the disaster. The eyewitness was a 17-year-old boy known as Pliny the Younger. His uncle, Pliny the Elder, was the commander of the Roman fleet stationed near Pompeii.

Pliny the Elder was also a scientist. After Vesuvius erupted, he died trying to get a closer look at the eruption. Pliny the Younger remained behind and observed the volcano from a safe distance of about 20 miles (32 kilometers) away. He writes that the ground had been shaking for days before the eruption. This happened so often that it did not panic the people of the area.

The eruption of Vesuvius spelled horror and sudden death for more than 2,000 people who were unable to flee. For historians, however, the disaster was a gift. When excavators discovered Pompeii 1,700 years later,

In Pompeii, a person could get a hot meal in one of the town's many food shops (left) or stop at a bakery for a loaf of bread (below).

they found a time capsule preserved by volcanic ash. The ash had preserved people in frozen poses, allowing historians to study how they had lived. Much of what we know about the Roman way of life comes from studying the remains of Pompeii.

In the ruins, excavators found the remains of bodies. The flesh was gone, leaving bones and hollow impressions in the hardened rock. **Archaeologists,** scientists who study the remains of peoples and cultures of the past, filled these spaces with liquid plaster. These plaster casts showed what people looked like at the moment of death. Among the saddest finds were a woman holding a baby and a boy with his pet dog.

The Streets of Pompeii

Walking the streets of Pompeii today, you can get a good idea of what the Roman way of life was like in Pliny the Younger's time. Pompeii's streets—even its busy main street—were narrow. They were just wide enough for donkey carts, judging by the ruts left in the old stone blocks. Each street was raised in the middle to permit water to run off into sewers. On a summer morning, Pliny would have smelled the stink of the sewers mixed with the aroma of fresh-baked bread from Pompeii's many bakeries.

THE NEXT BIG ONE?

Scientists who study Vesuvius say the volcano is still quite dangerous. A blast on the scale of the A.D. 79 eruption would devastate everything within four miles (six kilometers). Today, about one million people live in this zone. A Swiss scientist named Bernard Chouet has developed a way to predict a volcanic eruption if a certain type of earthquake activity is detected. Using his methods, scientists in Mexico City were able to predict an eruption in 2000 and thousands of people were moved to safety.

Pliny would have seen men in *togas*, the loose outer robe adult Roman males wore in public. The Roman women wore robes known as *stolas*. Both men and women wore sandals as they strolled along the narrow raised sidewalks. Some people had dogs with them. Little girls carried dolls, and boys played marbles. Pliny might pause at the family-owned stores where shopkeepers sold their many wares—sandals, pottery, dishes, tools, bottles of perfume, oil lamps, and blankets.

In his walk, Pliny would have passed one of the *thermopolia*, or fast-food restaurants, that were on every block. Large pots of stew and jugs of wine were set on a marble countertop. Food was kept warm by pots of hot water underneath. If he was feeling thirsty, he could stop at one of the stone water fountains found on many street corners. The water was carried in lead pipes running under the sidewalks. Wealthy people had running water in their homes.

At the Forum

Passing by one of Pompeii's two theaters, Pliny might hear actors rehearsing for that evening's performance or a poet practicing on his lyre. This was a stringed instrument similar to a harp that poets used to accompany themselves. Following the main street to the end, Pliny would reach the **forum**. In this public plaza,

Wall paintings in Pompeii's fine houses (left) show the cultivated lives of the city's wealthy women, who wore fine jewelry (below) like this necklace of pearls and precious stones.

he might meet his friends to talk and discuss business and politics. Lined with stone columns, the forum housed stalls from which merchants sold their goods. In the *macellum* (or market hall) there, the people of Pompeii could buy fish, meat, fruits, and vegetables.

The temple of Jupiter, one of ten temples in the city, stood at one end of the forum. At the other end, was one of Pompeii's three public baths. People socialized there while they cleaned up and exercised. In the distance, Pliny could hear the shouts of the crowd watching gladiators fight. Pompeii's amphitheater could seat 20,000 spectators. You can visit the amphitheater today and see Mount Vesuvius looming over the sports arena.

Pliny and the fight spectators would have seen the mountain as well, but they could not have guessed how it would destroy their city.

▶ *For more information about the legacy of Rome, see page 62.*

▶ *For more information about the legacy of Rome, see page 62.*

WHY IT MATTERS TODAY

Much of what we know about the daily life of the ancient Romans comes from studying the remains of Pompeii and the other towns buried by the eruption of Mount Vesuvius in A.D. 79. This disaster has proved to be an important resource for archaeologists and historians.

One of the ancient Romans' most important and enduring achievements was the development of design elements and construction methods that allowed them to create large, beautiful buildings.

ROME
Was Not Built in a Day

"What's the rush?" people often say to someone in a hurry. "Rome wasn't built in a day, you know!" The Romans were some of the greatest builders of all time, but they still had to do it brick by brick. The city of Rome was a great feat of engineering. Its public buildings were both beautiful and massive. To build them, the Romans needed new construction methods, interesting designs—and plenty of time.

The Romans' buildings rank among their greatest achievements. Some still stand, including the most famous Roman building of all, the Colosseum.

This stadium in Rome got its name from the Colossus, a gigantic statue of the emperor Nero that once stood nearby. The Colosseum was big too. It seated 50,000 people, and its walls towered 160 feet (49 meters) above the streets around it. Used for games, combats, and performances, the Colosseum was one of the most important gathering places in Rome. Spectators entered through one of 80 entrances and went to assigned seats. An entire crowd could be seated within a few minutes.

The Colosseum appears lower right in a model of the ancient city of Rome at the Museo della Civiltà Romana in Rome.

Building the Colosseum

Romans used one of their greatest inventions—concrete—for the Colosseum's main building material. The Romans wet the concrete and poured it into molds. Concrete was lighter than stone and could be made in larger, more irregular shapes than bricks.

The most important element in the design of the Colosseum was its many curved **arches.** The Colosseum's exterior includes dozens of arches.

The great advantage of an arch is its strength. If the top of a doorway is flat, the weight it supports may sometimes crack it. Arches can support more weight without cracking.

While guards keep watch, a lion climbs a ramp to the arena floor.

The ruins of the Colosseum

To build an arch, Roman builders first made a slightly smaller arch out of wood. Then they placed moist concrete around it. When the concrete was dry, they removed the wood. The result was a perfect concrete arch, strong and sturdy.

The walkways of the Colosseum were covered by curved, archlike ceilings known as **vaults.** The Colosseum's vaults were made of concrete too. They were stronger than wood ceilings and did not catch fire.

Building a structure the size of the Colosseum required tens of thousands of workers. These workers used several kinds of tools. To check that walls were straight, they used plumb lines—weights tied to pieces of string. To hoist materials to the top of the walls, Roman workers used a device called the great wheel, which looked like a large hamster wheel. They climbed into the wheel and turned it, allowing an attached crank to lift heavy loads into the air.

Just how long did it take to build Rome? Much longer than a day. The Colosseum alone took about ten years to build! But 2,000 years later, ruins still stand. An old saying warns that, "When the Colosseum falls, also ends Rome; and when Rome falls, the world will end."

SPORTS STADIUMS

Many modern stadiums reflect designs used in the ancient Roman Colosseum. Modern colosseums include the Silverdome in Pontiac, Michigan, and the RCA Dome in Indianapolis, Indiana. Both domes have roofs made of fabric, as did the ancient stadium.

The Romans had to use a system of ropes and poles to stretch canvas across their stadium. Thanks to engineering techniques, the modern roofs are held up by air pressure alone.

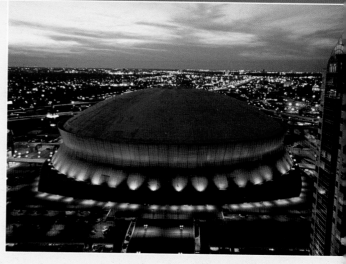

The Louisiana Superdome in New Orleans

ROMAN FACES

The ancient Romans were practical people. They were realistic too. In their art, they showed truthful images of people and how they lived. The portrait sculptures and paintings here preserve some of the kinds of faces you might have seen if you had lived in ancient Rome.

Roman aqueduct

Waterworks

The Romans' skill as engineers and builders was applied to other types of structures. Two of the most impressive kinds both dealt with water, aqueducts and public baths.

A Roman aqueduct was a channel used to bring water down from highland areas to cities. Usually, these water channels ran at ground level or below. But when an aqueduct had to cross low ground, such as a river or valley, Roman builders raised the channel on high arches.

Gravity gave tremendous force to the water flowing through these aqueducts. After traveling 20 miles (32 kilometers) downhill, the water that came barreling into a Roman city had such force that it would burst any pipe. To relieve the pressure, the Romans usually built great fountains at the point where the aqueduct entered the city. The most famous fountain in Europe, the Trevi Fountain in Rome, actually marks the end of an ancient 13-mile (21-kilometer) aqueduct. Some Roman aqueducts still function today.

Rome's earliest public baths were merely places to get clean. But the first

Roman emperors began building luxury spas with hot and cold pools for bathing and swimming, steam rooms, exercise courts and playing fields, libraries, gardens, and shops. Slaves stoked underground fires to provide heat, which was carried through floor and wall ducts. Central heating was another Roman invention.

▶ *For more information about the legacy of Rome, see page 62.*

WHY IT MATTERS TODAY

Roman architecture has remained an important influence on the design of buildings ever since. This influence can be strongly seen in many American government buildings, such as the U.S. Capitol. (The word *capitol* itself comes the name of one of Rome's seven hills.)

The Glory
of Rome

Jefferson Memorial in Washington, D.C.

Although invaders overthrew the Western Roman Empire some 1,500 years ago, Rome lives on in our architecture, government, arts, literature, and language.

Architecture

Would you like to see an example of Roman architecture in America? Look no further than the back of a nickel. The domed building pictured is Monticello, home of President Thomas Jefferson. He and the other founders of our country had great respect for Roman architecture because of its balance, harmony, and dignity. They used Roman design elements in many of our public buildings. Although the ancient Roman buildings themselves are in ruins today, modern builders still use the arch, the dome, the column, and concrete to create large, solid, and impressive structures.

The U.S. Senate and House of Representatives meet in a joint session of Congress.

Government

If you ever voted for a class president, you were following a Roman practice. Rome was governed by representatives elected by the people and responsible to them. The U.S. Senate and House of Representatives are based on that model. Another Roman feature in our government is the system of **checks and balances.** One example is the impeachment process. In it, one part of the government can get rid of a leader in another part who has abused power or committed crimes. This helps the different parts of government keep a check on each other's power.

You Too Can Speak Latin

The Romans spoke a language called Latin, and English has imported many words unchanged from the Latin language. Below are only a few of them.

subpoena	persona	virus
circa	bona fide	vice versa

On the back of every nickel is the Latin motto of the United States: *E Pluribus Unum*, meaning "out of many, one." Many countries use Latin words for medical, scientific, and legal terms. And if you ever read your horoscope in the newspaper, you will see the Latin names for zodiac signs, such as Leo, Taurus, Aries, and Cancer.

Laws

You might be familiar with many of our standards of justice from watching television programs about law and order. Some of the most important principles that we have borrowed from Rome are these:

- Laws must be adaptable to changing conditions.
- An accused person should be given a trial by a jury.
- An accused person should be defended by a lawyer.

Language

The Roman influence on the English language is as basic as ABC. The Roman alphabet is now the most widely used writing system in the world. The Romans spoke Latin, and Latin remained the language of learning long after the fall of Rome. The Roman Catholic Church continued to use Latin as its official language until the 1960s. Latin also developed into the modern *Romance* ("Roman") languages of French, Spanish, Portuguese, Italian, and Romanian. Even though English is not a Romance language, more than half of its words have a basis in Latin. For example, in the opening of the Declaration of Independence, "When in the course of human events," the words *course*, *human*, and *events* all come from Latin. So do *declaration* and *independence*.

Literature

Roman influences can be seen in a great deal of English literature. Writers from Shakespeare to 20th-century novelists have borrowed plots from Roman dramas, and even several modern Broadway musicals have featured Roman characters. Many historical movies tell the stories of ancient Romans from slaves to emperors. Have you ever seen a television show featuring twins that people get mixed up? That idea appeared in Roman literature long ago.

Daily Culture

We live with the legacy, or inheritance, of Rome every day. All the months of the year have Latin names, with January, March, and June named directly for the Roman gods Janus, Mars, and Juno.

The Roman gods also lend their names to all the planets of our solar system except Earth. Saturn does double duty as a day of the week (Saturday). The same gods have been used to sell products from candy bars to automobiles. And everyone knows Cupid, the little winged god with a bow and arrow who is so popular on Valentine's Day.

▶ *For more information about the legacy of Rome, see page 62.*

WHY IT MATTERS TODAY

The Western Roman Empire collapsed, but Rome's legacy to our world is so large and enduring that it is possible to say that Rome never really "fell."

Love

Ancient Rome

This Overview provides a brief summary of the most important people, places, and events of ancient Rome. Its purpose is to help you better understand the historical background of the articles in this book.

The Geography of Italy

The geography of Italy helped Rome gain power as a political, military, and economic center. Rich farmland, a good climate, and fish from the sea supplied plentiful food. The Alps, mountains to the north, formed a natural barrier. The Mediterranean Sea to the east, south, and west offered protection from enemies as well as easy access to trade routes.

By the 700s B.C., people known as the Latins were farming and raising cattle in west-central Italy. Seven hills, clustered along the Tiber River, drew other peoples, such as the Etruscans and the Sabines. Towns built on the seven hills traded with one another. The Tiber provided easy access to the sea and trade with the Greeks and other Mediterranean cultures.

The Founding of Rome

According to Roman legend, the Trojan prince Aeneas survived the destruction of Troy by the Greeks. He reached the seven hills along the Tiber that later would become Rome. His descendants, the twin boys Romulus and Remus, were cared for by a she-wolf after being abandoned as infants. In 753 B.C., Romulus founded the city of Rome, named it for himself, and became its first king.

Major Events

753 B.C.
Rome founded

218 B.C.
Hannibal
invades Italy

1000 B.C.

500 B.C

509 B.C.
Roman Republic
established

312 B.C.
Appian Way
begun

146 B.C.
Rome destroys
Carthage

Romulus and Remus

The Etruscans

A highly civilized people who lived north of Rome, the Etruscans strongly influenced early Roman development. The Romans based their Latin alphabet on the Etruscan writing system and adopted the toga and short cloak worn by the Etruscans. The Romans also borrowed elements of Etruscan architecture, particularly the arch, and Etruscan military organization. Rome's final rulers were Etruscans. In about 509 B.C., the brutal rule of the last of these kings, known as Tarquin the Proud, led to a revolt.

Tarquin and his family were expelled from Rome and upper-class Romans set up a republic—a government of elected officials.

Patricians and Plebeians

In the Roman Republic, struggles over political power between the aristocrats and working people were common. Members of upper-class, wealthy Roman families were known as patricians. Other citizens were called plebeians (plih–BEE–uhns). In the early days of the Republic, patricians selected leaders from among their own people. Plebeians were forbidden to hold office or even to marry a patrician. In 494 B.C., the plebeians marched out of Rome. They threatened to start a city of their own. Faced with no one to do their work, the patricians agreed that the plebeians could be represented by a new official called a tribune.

Roman Law

In the early republic, Roman law was unwritten. The patricians in power could change the laws to suit themselves. The plebeians now demanded that laws be written down. In about 451 B.C., Rome's first set of written laws was painted on 12 flat pieces of wood and hung up in the Forum. The laws of the Twelve Tables covered everything from trials to burials.

27 B.C.
Augustus becomes emperor

A.D. 122
Hadrian's Wall begun

A.D. 476
Fall of the Western Roman Empire

A.D. 1

A.D. 500

44 B.C.
Julius Caesar murdered

A.D. 313
Constantine grants freedom of worship

The Roman Republic

The Roman Army

During the republic, the Roman army was a militia, that is, a military force of ordinary citizens called up to serve during a particular conflict. Roman soldiers usually returned home when the war was over, but they could be called up again until they had served for a total of 16 years.

During the empire, the army became much more professional. Soldiers were nearly all volunteers who served a fixed term of 16 (later 25) years.

The Punic Wars

Carthage, a major trading center on the north coast of Africa, controlled trade on the Mediterranean Sea through its navy. Rome was determined to conquer Carthage, but the Romans knew little about naval warfare. By contrast, Carthage was weaker in land-based warfare, relying on an army of hired soldiers. Between 264 and 146 B.C., Rome and Carthage fought the Punic Wars.

As a result of Rome's victory in the First Punic War, the Romans gained their first province, the island of Sicily. During the Second Punic War, the Carthaginian general Hannibal invaded Italy and crushed the Romans in a series of battles. However, he was unable to capture Rome itself, and was finally forced to return to Carthage, where the Romans defeated him in 202 B.C. In the Third Punic War, the Romans destroyed Carthage itself and sold its people into slavery.

Roman Society

Rome's conquests spread to Spain, Macedonia, Greece, and Asia Minor. The responsibility of ruling such a huge territory took its toll. Governors appointed by Rome angered the conquered peoples by imposing heavy taxes to pay the expenses of the Roman state. Greedy tax collectors filled their own pockets, and wealth poured into Rome. Newly rich Romans bought up small farms and used slave labor to operate their huge estates.

Romans defeat Hannibal's army at the Battle of Zama.

The death of Julius Caesar

Roman soldiers, away from their lands for many years in service of Rome, returned to find their property gone. The landless poor moved to Rome. There they lived crammed into unsanitary wooden apartment buildings. Disease and fire were commonplace. Hostility grew between the wealthy and the rest of the population. Slaves revolted. Roman citizens who once served Rome out of a sense of duty and honor now questioned the selfishness of their rulers. The Roman Republic was falling apart.

Civil War

Several members of the ruling class tried to resolve some of the problems. In 133 B.C., Tiberius Gracchus complained about the treatment of returning soldiers. Tiberius's brother, Gaius, proposed a plan to divide public lands among poor farmers. The brothers had the people's support, but Rome's upper class feared the loss of power and had the brothers killed.

The deaths of the brothers triggered a century of civil war. Generals found that having their own armies gave them great power. Sulla, who supported the upper class, marched on Rome. It was the first time that a Roman army had attacked its own people.

Sulla succeeded in gaining power, but once he left for more conquests, his rival Marius seized Rome and killed many of the Senate leaders. Sulla struck back and massacred more than 5,000 of the people's leaders. Who could save the shattered state?

Julius Caesar

Rome's continued existence as a world power was due in large part to Julius Caesar.

Caesar was both a successful military leader and a talented statesman. He saw the corruption of the current system and decided that it would take strong leadership to save Rome. By 46 B.C., Caesar had defeated his major enemies. He kept the appearance of a republic, but government was now in the hands of a single powerful ruler—Caesar.

Despite his many contributions to Rome's power and stability, Caesar's ambitions (goals) offended many. Sixty senators, including some of Caesar's closest friends, conspired to assassinate, or murder, him. Caesar's death in 44 B.C. marked the end of the Roman Republic and the beginning of the Roman Empire.

The Roman Empire

The Age of Augustus

In 29 B.C., Caesar's nephew and adopted son Octavian became the leader of Rome. He claimed to be restoring the rule of the people. But he actually created an empire under the rule of a single powerful leader. In 27 B.C., the Senate gave Octavian the title of *Augustus*—"Revered One." With control of the army, Augustus gave peace to a country tired of civil war.

Augustus beautified Rome, creating a city fit to rule an empire. He boasted that he "had found Rome brick and left it marble." By the time of his death in A.D. 14, Augustus had laid a solid foundation for the Roman Empire.

During the next 55 years, the empire survived a series of emperors, several of whom were brutal or unstable. The proud emperor Caligula once insulted the Senate by appointing his horse as consul, a high official position. Nero, rather than waiting for assassination, killed himself. In A.D. 69, order was finally reestablished when Vespasian became emperor.

Pax Romana

The *Pax Romana*, or "Roman Peace," that began under Augustus lasted for two centuries. Fighting took place only at the frontiers of the empire. Within Italy, strong local leaders held power in the provinces. Conquered peoples around the Mediterranean engaged in peaceful trade. The Romans built paved roads across Italy, Germany, France, and Britain. Roman aqueducts and bridges appeared throughout France, and Roman wells were seen in oases of the Sahara. Free people throughout the empire in growing numbers became Roman citizens, living by Roman law. The arts and literature were valued and encouraged. From A.D. 96 to 180, five men known as the

Augustus supported artists, including the poet Virgil (seated), the greatest Roman writer.

Early Christian art showing Jesus as the Good Shepherd

"Good Emperors" ruled the empire. Four of them were from Italian provinces outside Rome. The Good Emperors strengthened the defenses and internal government of the empire. The Roman Empire reached its largest size.

The Spread of Christianity

About A.D. 30, a Jewish spiritual leader named Jesus appeared in the Roman province of Judea. Although his message was one of peace rather than revolt, Roman officials thought that Jesus would endanger Roman rule by causing controversy. In A.D. 33, the Roman governor Pontius Pilate arrested Jesus and had him crucified, or hung from a cross until he died.

The death of Jesus strengthened the faith of his Jewish followers, who soon began to preach his message to non-Jews. The Christian message of love was not directed at the rich or powerful. Christians welcomed slaves and the poor into their community. Rome had a tradition of religious tolerance, so Christianity continued to spread. However, Romans felt that the Christian failure to worship Roman gods could undermine the empire. Christians began to be persecuted.

The Division of the Empire

In A.D. 180, Commodus, the son of the last "Good Emperor," turned the empire from "a kingdom of gold into one of iron and rust." Civil wars ended the *Pax Romana*. Germanic tribes in the west and the Persian Empire in the east threatened the empire's borders. Defending the empire stretched the finances and the military might of Rome. In 284, the emperor Diocletian divided the empire in two.

He ruled the eastern empire and appointed a co-emperor to rule the western empire. In 312, Constantine took power and reunited the empire. Constantine changed Roman history in two ways. First, he established a new capital city at Constantinople. Second, he issued an order granting freedom of religion to all people in the empire, including Christians. Christianity gradually replaced traditional worship of many gods.

Gold coin of the emperor Diocletian

The End of the Empire

Barbarian Invasions

In the late 300s, a new threat appeared from the east. The Huns, a fierce nomadic tribe, swarmed over Europe. One Roman historian said that the Huns "live on the roots of wild plants and the half-raw flesh of any sort of animal. . . They wear garments of the skins of field mice stitched together." The Huns drove the Germanic peoples who lived along the borders of the empire into Roman territory. Among these were the Visigoths and Ostragoths.

The Fall of Rome

In 410, Alaric, the king of the Visigoths, attacked and captured Rome itself. The Visigoths forced Rome to pay tribute to the Huns to keep them from attacking. But the Huns pushed more and more tribes into the Roman Empire. Finally, the Hun leader, Attila, marched on Rome itself. The only thing that kept the city from destruction was a plague, a kind of widespread disease. The leader of the Christian church, Pope Leo I,

Visigoths attacking Rome

convinced Attila to withdraw rather than risk his troops. The Huns left, but the Western Roman Empire was in ruins.

In 476, the last Western Roman emperor was overthrown. The Eastern Roman Empire, ruled from Constantinople, would survive. But the city of Rome was no longer the capital of an empire. Some historians believe that the fall of the empire had begun long before the city of Rome fell. In their view, Rome's decline began when the Roman people turned from lives of honor and dedication to lives in search

of luxury and power. Other historians say that the empire never ended, but gradually changed into the new power structure of the Middle Ages.

The Roman Legacy

Whatever happened to Rome and the Roman Empire, Roman contributions to culture remained. Languages such as French, Spanish, Romanian, and Portuguese have their roots in Latin, as do many English words. During the great days of the empire, many countries of Europe followed Roman law. As these countries colonized other continents, they carried Roman legal practices with them. Architecture and engineering are influenced by Roman arches, bridges, roads, and aqueducts. Poetry, plays, and history by Roman writers remain as great works of literature. The Roman Empire may have ended, but its legacy remains throughout the world.

GLOSSARY

aqueduct a channel used to carry water

arch a curved structure that spans an open space and supports weight

archaeologist a scientist who studies the remains of peoples and cultures of the past

auxiliary a soldier recruited from lands the Romans had conquered

century a unit of 80 to 100 men in the Roman army, commanded by a centurion

checks and balances a system by which the divisions of government keep each other from becoming too powerful

cohort a unit of about 480 men in the Roman army

dictator a Roman leader given complete power in an emergency

forum the public meeting place of a Roman city

legion the major unit of the ancient Roman army, consisting of 4,000 to 5,000 men, called legionaries

missionary a person who works to spread a religion

persecution cruel treatment, especially because of politics, religion, or race

province a division of the Roman Empire outside the city of Rome

republic a form of government in which citizens elect their leaders

Senate the supreme council of state in the Roman Republic

vault a curved, archlike ceiling

Roman silver cup decorated with skeletons reflects the famous Roman motto *Carpe diem*, "Seize the day"—live for the moment.

INDEX